Broken
Promises

Sometimes, people make promises they can't keep—even parents. Sometimes, your parents aren't there for you when you need them, even when they say they will be. It can be tough, because you should be able to trust your parents to keep their word, but sometimes they don't. Sometimes they might disappoint you, or make you mad. Use this book to help you recognize and handle these feelings, and remember that no matter what, YOU are an AWESOME kid!

Draw a picture of your family in the box below.

In the boxes below, describe each of your family members.

My Family Member	This person is...

What are some of your favorite things about
your family?

_____

_____

_____

_____

_____

What are some of your least favorite things about
your family?

_____

_____

_____

_____

_____

Sometimes, parents break their promises and let you down. It's okay to feel disappointed when this happens, and it can help to talk about it. Share some of the times you've been let down by your parent.

"The person who lets me down is _____"

"My parent let me down when..."
(Describe some examples in the shapes below.)

"My parent let me down when..."
(Describe some examples in the shapes below.)

When a parent breaks a promise, you may have many different feelings. Add your feelings to the circles below alongside those already mentioned.

Angry

Disappointed

How broken promises make me feel

When you have all these feelings, sometimes it can be confusing, so it may help you to talk to someone about them. Write the names of people you can talk to in the boxes below.

Draw

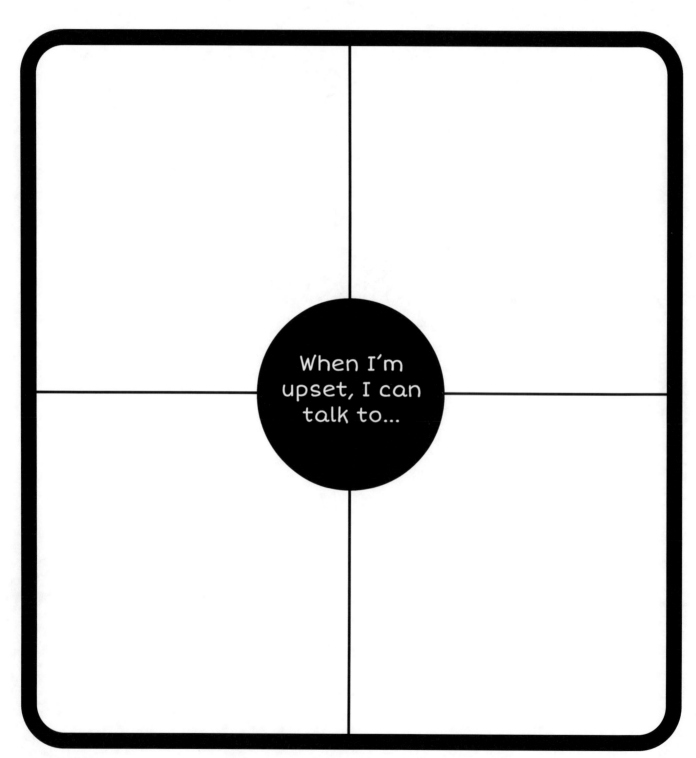

When I'm upset, I can talk to...

Sometimes, you're not sure how you feel. You can have a lot of feelings all mixed up inside you at the same time, and it can be hard to use words to describe them. Instead, try drawing your feelings in the box below. Use many colors to help get all your different feelings out.

It's ok to feel angry or disappointed. We can't always control our feelings, but we can control how we respond to them. Sometimes, when we feel angry or disappointed, we may say or do things we shouldn't. Instead, we need to figure out healthy way to deal with out feelings.

Let's work on some healthy ways to deal with your feelings.
What are some good things you can do when you're feeling
upset? Write them in the circle below.

When you're going through a tough time, it can help to remember happy times. Think about some good memories you have with your parent, and write about them in the sun shapes below.

Pick one of the happy memories you wrote about and draw it in the box below. Use this happy time to remember that your parent loves you.

List three things you love about your parent. Remember these things when you're upset.

1. _____

2. _____

3. _____

Broken Promises

My dad makes me promises he doesn't keep.
He say he'll be there to tuck me in to sleep.
But then nighttime comes and he isn't home,
And I lie down feeling very alone.

This weekend, he tells me, we'll finally play
Whatever I want, we'll spend the whole day.
But when Saturday comes, he doesn't come through
Making excuses is all he can do.

When my dad lets me down, I feel angry and sad.
It makes me feel lonely; it makes me feel bad.
Sometimes I feel like he just doesn't care,
When he breaks his word and when he isn't there.

I have to remember when my heart aches
That even grownups can make mistakes.
I know that he loves me and it's not my fault
I'm still a great kid, no matter what.

Do you see any similarities between what has happened to you and what has happened to the kid in the poem? Write about them below.

_____

_____

Circle words in the poem on the previous page that illustrate how you feel. Use the space below to draw a picture of the poem, as well as how it relates to your own feelings. In the poem, the kid's father has promised to spend time with her, but he doesn't show up. If this ever happens to you, it can be very disappointing, but you should know that you're great all on your own and you know how to do lots of cool things. So instead of just being sad and lonely, find something fun to do on your own! In the boxes below, write some ideas for fun things you can do when you're spending time by yourself.

It can help to know you're not the only person who has ever felt this way. There are lots of kids out there whose parents break their word and aren't always there for them. There are also a lot of kids like that in books, movies, and TV shows. Can you think of any characters with parents who have let them down? How did those kids handle it? Write about them in the boxes below.

Character	How He or She Handled the Problem

Pick one of the
characters you wrote
about on the previous
page and draw him
or her in the star.

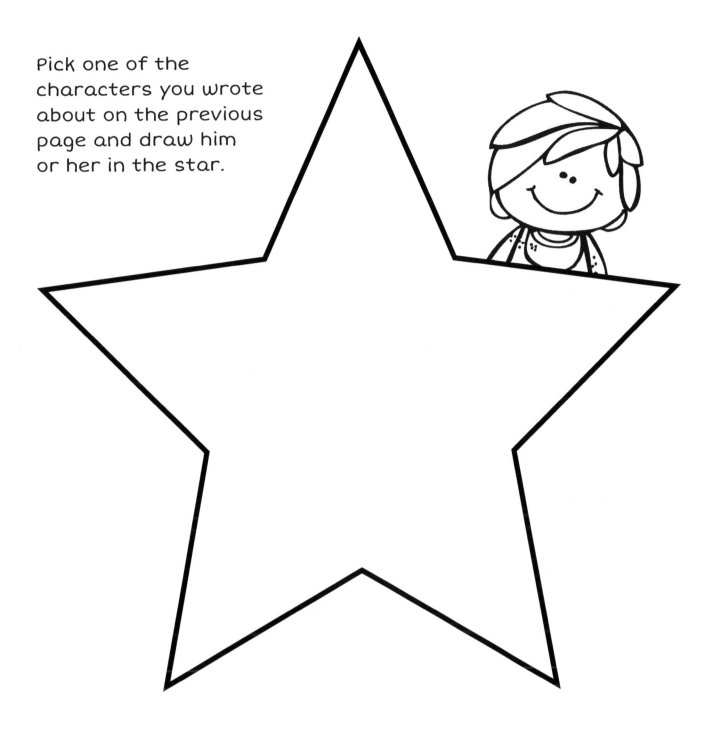

What advice do you think this character might have for you in
your situation?

_____

_____

_____

When parents break promises, they often have excuses. When this happens over and over, though, the excuse aren't good enough. In the speech bubbles, write some excuses you've heard from your parent.

How does it make you feel when your parent makes excuses?

_____

_____

_____

You are a great kid, and deserve to be treated like one. Read the excuses on the previous page, then cross them out. You deserve better than these excuses! In the scroll, write how you deserve to be treated.

It can help to talk to your parent about what makes you feel upset. Your parent might not even realize how hurt you are! In the boxes below, write down the things your parent does that upset you. Imagine you're talking to your parent when you write them.

"When you _____,

I feel _____ because _____

_____

"When you _____,

I feel _____ because _____

_____

"When you _____,

I feel _____ because _____

_____

Now practice saying these sentences in a calm voice. When you're feeling brave enough, try saying them to your parent.

When things are hard, it can help to think about the future and things getting better. Even if all our wishes don't always come true, having hope and something to look forward to can help us get through hard times. What would you wish for? Write your wishes in these clouds.

Pick one of your wishes and illustrate it in the box below.

You're over halfway through this book. Congratulations! You've been really brave and strong, so let's take a look at how far you've come. Fill out the first two boxes with your feelings before starting this book, and your feelings now. After you've completed this whole book, come back to this page and write about your feelings in the last box.

Before starting this book, when my parent would let me down, I felt...

Now I feel...

After completing this book, I feel...

When your parent lets you down, it's important to remember that it's not your fault. It doesn't mean your parent doesn't love you, or there's something wrong with you. You're still an awesome kid! Help yourself remember that you're an awesome kid by writing good things about yourself in the banners below.

Draw a picture of yourself doing something you're good at.

This is just one of the many things that
make you a great kid!

It's also important to remember that there are lots of other people who love you, too. These people can help you when you're feeling lonely or upset. Write the names of people who care about you in the hearts.

These people think you're great! What good things would they say about you? Write those things in the speech bubbles below. If you're not sure what to write, ask the people who love you!

Sometimes, your parent might say or do things that hurt your feelings. Remember: It's not your fault! When this happens, help yourself be strong by thinking about the good things about yourself. In the speech bubbles below, write something your parents has said or done that upset you. In the thought bubbles, write something good you can tell yourself when this happens.

If you could say anything to your parent, what would it be? Write a letter to him or her below. If you want, share it with your parent. Sometimes writing about how you feel is easier than saying it out loud.

Dear _____

_____

_____

_____

_____

_____

_____

_____

_____

Love,

_____

Have you ever made a mistake? Well, grownups make mistakes, too—even parents! When you make a mistake, you want people to forgive you. Sometimes, when people forgive each other, you'll hear them say, "That's okay." This is not really what forgiveness means, though. Forgiveness does not make what was done to you okay—forgiveness means that you're choosing to let go of your anger about what happened. Forgiveness helps you as much as the person you're forgiving, if not more! Forgiving someone who has hurt you is not always easy, but it can be an important step in moving forward.

Why is it sometimes hard to forgive?

_____

_____

_____

_____

Why is it important to try to forgive?

_____

_____

_____

_____

Draw

Forgiveness is about letting go of your anger. In the box below, let your anger out: Draw, scribble, or write whatever you need to get your feelings out. Then, when you're ready, draw a huge X across the paper and say, "I forgive you."

Forgiveness can also mean showing love to people, even when they haven't treated us right. In the hearts, write or draw four ways you can show love to your parent.

You've learned a lot of great ways to deal with your feelings when your parent lets you down. All these strategies are your tools to help you get through hard times. Write down these tools inside the toolbox below to help you remember.

MY TOOLS

You've come a long way. You should be proud of yourself. You're becoming very strong. This doesn't mean there will never be any more tough times, but it does mean that when tough times come, you'll be ready for them. When things get hard, remind yourself about everything you've learned in this book and how great you are. Write a letter to yourself below. When you're going through a hard time, pull this letter out and read it to yourself as a reminder.

Dear _____

_____

_____

_____

_____

_____

_____

_____

_____

Love,

_____

Draw a picture of yourself in the space below, and write your name in the banner to remind yourself that YOU'RE AN AWESOME KID!

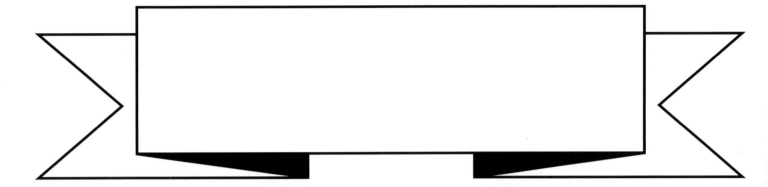

Great job! You've made it through this book and learned a lot about yourself and how to deal with your feelings when things at home get hard. Keep this book to help you remember everything you've learned. Take it out whenever you need to get your feelings out, or when you need a reminder that you're an awesome kid.

HOW TO USE THIS REFLECTION JOURNAL

Now that you've completed the activities in this workbook, it's time to focus on putting everything you learned into practice.

What does that mean? It means using the things you've learned to help you each day.

Make a plan for each morning; then at the end of the day, before bedtime, think about your day.

What was good about it?
What brought you joy?
What went wrong?
How did you handle it?
What can you do to have a great day tomorrow?

HOW TO USE THIS REFLECTION JOURNAL

STEP 1: Each morning make a plan for your day by completing Side 1 of that day's journal page.

STEP 2: Each evening complete side 2 as you reflect on your day.

DATE: S M T W TH F S ___/___/___

ONLY POSITIVE THOUGHTS IN MY DAY
I can make today awesome by:

_____

_____

_____

DRAW IT!

what are you looking forward to most today?

I LOVE MYSELF
LIST 3 THINGS YOU LOVE ABOUT YOURSELF

WHAT IS SOMETHING THAT MAKES YOU HAPPY

_____

_____

_____

TODAY I FELT

SOMETHING GREAT THAT HAPPENED TODAY

_____

_____

_____

 THIS PERSON BROUGHT ME JOY TODAY

_____

_____

DATE: S M T W TH F S ___/___/___

ONLY POSITIVE THOUGHTS IN MY DAY
I can make today awesome by:

_____

_____

_____

DRAW IT!

what are you looking forward to most today?

I LOVE MYSELF
LIST 3 words that describe you

WHAT DO YOU LIKE TO DO FOR FUN

_____

_____

_____

TODAY I FELT

SOMETHING GREAT THAT HAPPENED TODAY

_____

_____

_____

 THIS PERSON BROUGHT ME JOY TODAY

_____

_____

DATE: S M T W TH F S ___/___/___

ONLY POSITIVE THOUGHTS IN MY DAY

I can make today awesome by:

_____

_____

_____

DRAW IT!

what are you looking forward to most today?

I LOVE MYSELF

LIST 3 THINGS you are really good at doing

WHAT IS ONE OF YOUR FAVORITE MEMORIES

_____

_____

_____

TODAY I FELT

SOMETHING GREAT THAT HAPPENED TODAY

_____

_____

_____

 THIS PERSON BROUGHT ME JOY TODAY

_____

_____

DATE: S M T W TH F S ___/___/___

ONLY POSITIVE THOUGHTS IN MY DAY

I can make today awesome by:

_____

_____

_____

DRAW IT!

what are you looking forward to most today?

I LOVE MYSELF

LIST 3 THINGS YOU LOVE doing

WHO IS A PERSON YOU ADMIRE (LIKE)

_____

_____

_____

TODAY I FELT

SOMETHING GREAT THAT HAPPENED TODAY

_____

_____

_____

 THIS PERSON BROUGHT ME JOY TODAY

_____

_____

DATE: S M T W TH F S ___/___/___

ONLY POSITIVE THOUGHTS IN MY DAY

I can make today awesome by:

_____

_____

_____

DRAW IT!

what are you looking forward to most today?

I LOVE MYSELF

LIST 3 THINGS YOU'D LIKE to improve about yourself

WHAT IS SOMETHING THAT MAKES YOU PROUD?

_____

_____

_____

TODAY I FELT

SOMETHING GREAT THAT HAPPENED TODAY

_____

_____

_____

 THIS PERSON BROUGHT ME JOY TODAY

_____

_____

DATE: S M T W TH F S ___/___/___

ONLY POSITIVE THOUGHTS IN MY DAY
I can make today awesome by:

_____

_____

_____

DRAW IT!

what are you looking forward to most today?

I LOVE MYSELF
LIST 3 THINGS THAT BRING YOU HAPPINESS

WHO IS THE KINDEST PERSON YOU KNOW

_____

_____

_____

TODAY I FELT

SOMETHING GREAT THAT HAPPENED TODAY

_____

_____

_____

 THIS PERSON BROUGHT ME JOY TODAY

_____

_____

DATE: S M T W TH F S ___/___/___

ONLY POSITIVE THOUGHTS IN MY DAY
I can make today awesome by:

_____

_____

_____

DRAW IT!

what are you looking forward to most today?

I LOVE MYSELF
WRITE 3 WORDS TO DESCRIBE YOUR LIFE

DID I TRY SOMETHING NEW TODAY?

_____

_____

_____

TODAY I FELT

SOMETHING GREAT THAT HAPPENED TODAY

_____

_____

_____

 THIS PERSON BROUGHT ME JOY TODAY

_____

_____

DATE: S M T W TH F S ___/___/___

ONLY POSITIVE THOUGHTS IN MY DAY

I can make today awesome by:

_____

_____

_____

DRAW IT!

what are you looking forward to most today?

I LOVE MYSELF

LIST 3 THINGS WORDS TO DESCRIBE YOUR FAMILY

DID I GET OUT OF MY COMFORT ZONE TODAY?

_____

_____

_____

TODAY I FELT

SOMETHING GREAT THAT HAPPENED TODAY

_____

_____

_____

 THIS PERSON BROUGHT ME JOY TODAY

_____

_____

DATE: S M T W TH F S ___/___/___

ONLY POSITIVE THOUGHTS IN MY DAY
I can make today awesome by:

_____

_____

_____

DRAW IT!

what are you looking forward to most today?

I LOVE MYSELF
LIST 3 THINGS YOU LOVE ABOUT YOURSELF

THIS IS WHAT I COULD HAVE DONE BETTER TODAY

_____

_____

_____

TODAY I FELT

SOMETHING GREAT THAT HAPPENED TODAY

_____

_____

_____

 THIS PERSON BROUGHT ME JOY TODAY

_____

_____

DATE: S M T W TH F S ___/___/___

ONLY POSITIVE THOUGHTS IN MY DAY
I can make today awesome by:

_____

_____

_____

DRAW IT!
what are you looking forward to most today?

I LOVE MYSELF
LIST 3 THINGS THAT MAKE YOU SMILE

TODAY I LEARNED THIS ABOUT MYSELF

_____

_____

_____

TODAY I FELT

SOMETHING GREAT THAT HAPPENED TODAY

_____

_____

_____

THIS PERSON BROUGHT ME JOY TODAY

_____

_____

DATE: S M T W TH F S ___/___/___

ONLY POSITIVE THOUGHTS IN MY DAY

I can make today awesome by:

_____

_____

_____

DRAW IT!

what are you looking forward to most today?

I LOVE MYSELF

WRITE 3 THINGS THAT ARE GREAT ABOUT YOU

WHAT I'M LOVING ABOUT LIFE RIGHT NOW

_____

_____

_____

TODAY I FELT

SOMETHING GREAT THAT HAPPENED TODAY

_____

_____

_____

 THIS PERSON BROUGHT ME JOY TODAY

_____

_____

DATE: S M T W TH F S ___/___/___

ONLY POSITIVE THOUGHTS IN MY DAY

I can make today awesome by:

_____

_____

_____

DRAW IT!

what are you looking forward to most today?

I LOVE MYSELF

NAME 3 PEOPLE WHO BRING YOU HAPPINESS

I HOPE TOMORROW LOOKS LIKE THIS

_____

_____

_____

TODAY I FELT

SOMETHING GREAT THAT HAPPENED TODAY

_____

_____

_____

 THIS PERSON BROUGHT ME JOY TODAY

_____

_____

DATE: S M T W TH F S ___/___/___

ONLY POSITIVE THOUGHTS IN MY DAY
I can make today awesome by:

_____

_____

_____

DRAW IT!

what are you looking forward to most today?

I LOVE MYSELF
NAME 3 THINGS YOUR FRIENDS THINK YOU ARE AWESOME AT

_____

_____

_____

TODAY I FELT

SOMETHING GREAT THAT HAPPENED TODAY

_____

_____

_____

 THIS PERSON BROUGHT ME JOY TODAY

_____

_____

DATE: S M T W TH F S ___/___/___

ONLY POSITIVE THOUGHTS IN MY DAY
I can make today awesome by:

_____

_____

_____

DRAW IT!

what are you looking forward to most today?

I LOVE MYSELF
WRITE 3 THINGS YOUR CLASSMATES SAY YOU ARE GREAT AT

THIS IS WHAT I WANT TO IMPROVE ABOUT MYSELF

_____

_____

_____

TODAY I FELT

SOMETHING GREAT THAT HAPPENED TODAY

_____

_____

_____

THIS PERSON BROUGHT ME JOY TODAY

_____

_____

DATE: S M T W TH F S ___/___/___

ONLY POSITIVE THOUGHTS IN MY DAY

I can make today awesome by:

_____

_____

_____

DRAW IT!

what are you looking forward to most today?

I LOVE MYSELF

LIST 3 THINGS YOU DO THAT MAKES YOUR FAMILY HAPPY

TODAY I.....

_____

_____

_____

TODAY I FELT

SOMETHING GREAT THAT HAPPENED TODAY

_____

_____

_____

THIS PERSON BROUGHT ME JOY TODAY

_____

_____

DATE: S M T W TH F S ___/___/__

ONLY POSITIVE THOUGHTS IN MY DAY
I can make today awesome by:

_____

_____

_____

DRAW IT!

what are you looking forward to most today?

I LOVE MYSELF
LIST 3 THINGS THAT MAKE YOU HAPPY

WHAT I'M LOVING ABOUT LIFE RIGHT NOW

_____

_____

_____

TODAY I FELT

SOMETHING GREAT THAT HAPPENED TODAY

_____

_____

_____

 THIS PERSON BROUGHT ME JOY TODAY

_____

_____

DATE: S M T W TH F S ___/___/___

ONLY POSITIVE THOUGHTS IN MY DAY
I can make today awesome by:

_____

_____

_____

DRAW IT!

what are you looking forward to most today?

I LOVE MYSELF
LIST 3 THINGS THAT MAKE YOU FEEL GOOD

TODAY I WANT TO.....

_____

_____

_____

TODAY I FELT

SOMETHING GREAT THAT HAPPENED TODAY

_____

_____

_____

THIS PERSON BROUGHT ME JOY TODAY

_____

_____

DATE: S M T W TH F S ___/___/___

ONLY POSITIVE THOUGHTS IN MY DAY
I can make today awesome by:

_____

_____

_____

DRAW IT!

what are you looking forward to most today?

I LOVE MYSELF
LIST 3 FUTURE GOALS FOR YOURSELF

TODAY'S ACTIVITIES MADE ME.....

_____

_____

_____

TODAY I FELT

SOMETHING GREAT THAT HAPPENED TODAY

_____

_____

_____

THIS PERSON BROUGHT ME JOY TODAY

_____

_____

DATE: S M T W TH F S ___/___/___

ONLY POSITIVE THOUGHTS IN MY DAY
I can make today awesome by:

_____

_____

_____

DRAW IT!

what are you looking forward to most today?

I LOVE MYSELF
LIST 3 THINGS YOU ENJOY DOING

TODAY I WANTED TO....

_____

_____

_____

TODAY I FELT

SOMETHING GREAT THAT HAPPENED TODAY

_____

_____

_____

THIS PERSON BROUGHT ME JOY TODAY

_____

_____

DATE: S M T W TH F S ___/___/___

ONLY POSITIVE THOUGHTS IN MY DAY
I can make today awesome by:

_____

_____

_____

DRAW IT!

what are you looking forward to most today?

I LOVE MYSELF
LIST 3 THINGS YOU DO THAT MAKES OTHERS SMILE

IF I COULD CHANGE THIS ABOUT TODAY

_____

_____

_____

TODAY I FELT

SOMETHING GREAT THAT HAPPENED TODAY

_____

_____

_____

 ## THIS PERSON BROUGHT ME JOY TODAY

_____

_____

DATE: S M T W TH F S   ___/___/___

ONLY POSITIVE THOUGHTS IN MY DAY
I can make today awesome by:

_____

_____

_____

DRAW IT!
what are you looking forward to most today?

I LOVE MYSELF
LIST 3 THINGS YOU LOVE ABOUT YOURSELF

MY DAY WAS.....

_____

_____

_____

TODAY I FELT

SOMETHING GREAT THAT HAPPENED TODAY

_____

_____

_____

THIS PERSON BROUGHT ME JOY TODAY

_____

_____

DATE: S M T W TH F S ___/___/___

ONLY POSITIVE THOUGHTS IN MY DAY

I can make today awesome by:

_____

_____

_____

DRAW IT!

what are you looking forward to most today?

I LOVE MYSELF

WRITE 3 AFFIRMATIONS: I AM.....

I LEARNED THIS ABOUT MYSELF TODAY

_____

_____

_____

TODAY I FELT

SOMETHING GREAT THAT HAPPENED TODAY

_____

_____

_____

THIS PERSON BROUGHT ME JOY TODAY

_____

_____

DATE: S M T W TH F S ___/___/___

ONLY POSITIVE THOUGHTS IN MY DAY
I can make today awesome by:

_____

_____

_____

DRAW IT!

what are you looking forward to most today?

I LOVE MYSELF
LIST 3 GOALS YOU'D LIKE TO ACHIEVE THIS WEEK

I HOPE TOMORROW IS....

_____

_____

_____

TODAY I FELT

😊 🙂 😐 🙁 😣 😴

SOMETHING GREAT THAT HAPPENED TODAY

_____

_____

_____

THIS PERSON BROUGHT ME JOY TODAY

_____

_____

DATE: S M T W TH F S ___/___/___

ONLY POSITIVE THOUGHTS IN MY DAY
I can make today awesome by:

_____

_____

_____

DRAW IT!

what are you looking forward to most today?

I LOVE MYSELF
LIST 3 THINGS YOU HAVE ALWAYS WANTED TO DO

LIFE IS GOOD BECAUSE...

_____

_____

_____

TODAY I FELT

SOMETHING GREAT THAT HAPPENED TODAY

_____

_____

_____

THIS PERSON BROUGHT ME JOY TODAY

_____

_____

DATE: S M T W TH F S ___/___/___

ONLY POSITIVE THOUGHTS IN MY DAY

I can make today awesome by:

_____

_____

_____

DRAW IT!

what are you looking forward to most today?

I LOVE MYSELF

LIST 3 THINGS YOU DREAM ABOUT

```
_____ IS MY HERO
BECAUSE.....
```

_____

_____

_____

TODAY I FELT

SOMETHING GREAT THAT HAPPENED TODAY

_____

_____

_____

 ## THIS PERSON BROUGHT ME JOY TODAY

_____

_____

DATE: S M T W TH F S ___/___/___

ONLY POSITIVE THOUGHTS IN MY DAY

I can make today awesome by:

_____

_____

_____

DRAW IT!

what are you looking forward to most today?

I LOVE MYSELF

LIST 3 THINGS YOU HOPE TO DO THIS WEEK

TODAY I SMILED BECAUSE

_____

_____

_____

TODAY I FELT

SOMETHING GREAT THAT HAPPENED TODAY

_____

_____

_____

THIS PERSON BROUGHT ME JOY TODAY

_____

_____

DATE: S M T W TH F S ___/___/___

ONLY POSITIVE THOUGHTS IN MY DAY

I can make today awesome by:

_____

_____

_____

DRAW IT!

what are you looking forward to most today?

I LOVE MYSELF

LIST 3 THINGS YOU LOOK FORWARD TO

WHEN I FEEL MAD THIS IS WHAT I DO

_____

_____

_____

TODAY I FELT

SOMETHING GREAT THAT HAPPENED TODAY

_____

_____

_____

 ## THIS PERSON BROUGHT ME JOY TODAY

_____

_____

DATE: S M T W TH F S ___/___/___

ONLY POSITIVE THOUGHTS IN MY DAY

I can make today awesome by:

_____

_____

_____

DRAW IT!

what are you looking forward to most today?

I LOVE MYSELF

LIST 3 THINGS YOU DID THAT YOU WERE PROUD OF DOING

I'M GRATEFUL FOR

_____

_____

_____

TODAY I FELT

SOMETHING GREAT THAT HAPPENED TODAY

_____

_____

_____

THIS PERSON BROUGHT ME JOY TODAY

_____

_____

DATE: S M T W TH F S ___/___/___

ONLY POSITIVE THOUGHTS IN MY DAY

I can make today awesome by:

_____

_____

_____

DRAW IT!

what are you looking forward to most today?

I LOVE MYSELF

LIST 3 THINGS YOU ARE EXCITED ABOUT

WHAT I'M LOVING ABOUT LIFE RIGHT NOW

_____

_____

_____

TODAY I FELT

SOMETHING GREAT THAT HAPPENED TODAY

_____

_____

_____

 THIS PERSON BROUGHT ME JOY TODAY

_____

_____

DATE: S M T W TH F S ___/___/___

ONLY POSITIVE THOUGHTS IN MY DAY
I can make today awesome by:

_____

_____

_____

DRAW IT!

what are you looking forward to most today?

I LOVE MYSELF
LIST 3 THINGS YOU ARE THANKFUL FOR

MY FAVORITE PERSON TO BE AROUND IS

_____

_____

_____

TODAY I FELT

SOMETHING GREAT THAT HAPPENED TODAY

_____

_____

_____

 THIS PERSON BROUGHT ME JOY TODAY

_____

_____

DATE: S M T W TH F S ___/___/___

ONLY POSITIVE THOUGHTS IN MY DAY
I can make today awesome by:

_____

_____

_____

DRAW IT!
what are you looking forward to most today?

I LOVE MYSELF
LIST 3 WAYS YOUR LIFE IS AWESOME

THE PERSON I MOST ADMIRE IS

_____

_____

_____

TODAY I FELT

SOMETHING GREAT THAT HAPPENED TODAY

_____

_____

_____

THIS PERSON BROUGHT ME JOY TODAY

_____

_____

DATE: S M T W TH F S ___/___/___

ONLY POSITIVE THOUGHTS IN MY DAY
I can make today awesome by:

_____

_____

_____

DRAW IT!
what are you looking forward to most today?

I LOVE MYSELF
LIST 3 THINGS YOU DID THIS WEEK

THIS IS WHAT BRINGS ME HAPPINESS

_____

_____

_____

TODAY I FELT

SOMETHING GREAT THAT HAPPENED TODAY

_____

_____

_____

 ## THIS PERSON BROUGHT ME JOY TODAY

_____

_____

DATE: S M T W TH F S ___ / ___ / ___

ONLY POSITIVE THOUGHTS IN MY DAY
I can make today awesome by:

_____

_____

_____

DRAW IT!

what are you looking forward to most today?

I LOVE MYSELF
LIST 3 SMALL SUCCESS YOU HAD THIS WEEK

THIS ALWAYS MAKES ME SMILE

_____

_____

_____

TODAY I FELT

SOMETHING GREAT THAT HAPPENED TODAY

_____

_____

_____

 ## THIS PERSON BROUGHT ME JOY TODAY

_____

_____

DATE: S M T W TH F S ___/___/___

ONLY POSITIVE THOUGHTS IN MY DAY
I can make today awesome by:

_____

_____

_____

DRAW IT!
what are you looking forward to most today?

I LOVE MYSELF
LIST 3 THINGS YOU LIKE ABOUT YOURSELF

_____

_____

_____

TODAY I FELT

SOMETHING GREAT THAT HAPPENED TODAY

_____

_____

_____

THIS PERSON BROUGHT ME JOY TODAY

_____

_____

DATE: S M T W TH F S ___/___/___

ONLY POSITIVE THOUGHTS IN MY DAY
I can make today awesome by:

_____

_____

_____

DRAW IT!

what are you looking forward to most today?

I LOVE MYSELF
LIST 3 WORDS THAT DESCRIBE YOU

WHAT I'M LOOKING FORWARD TO TOMORROW

_____

_____

_____

TODAY I FELT

SOMETHING GREAT THAT HAPPENED TODAY

_____

_____

_____

THIS PERSON BROUGHT ME JOY TODAY

_____

_____

Made in the USA
Las Vegas, NV
03 December 2023

82012775R00061